Sniglets

RICH HALL & FRIENDS

Sniglets

(snig'lit) Any word that doesn't appear in the dictionary, but should

ANGUS
& ROBERTSON
PUBLISHERS

ANGUS & ROBERTSON PUBLISHERS

Unit 4, Eden Park, 31 Waterloo Road,
North Ryde, NSW, Australia 2113, and
16 Golden Square, London W1R 4BN,
United Kingdom

First published in Australia
by Angus & Robertson Publishers in 1988

Published by arrangement with Ebury Press

Copyright © 1984, 1985, 1986 by Not the Network Company Inc

Designed by Harry Green
Illustrations by Arnie Ten

ISBN 0 207 15742 1

Typeset by MFK Typesetting Ltd, Hitchin
Printed in Great Britain at the University Press, Cambridge
First published by Macmillan Publishing Company, New York

Contents

A

Accordionated
(ah kor' de on ay tid)

adj. Being able to drive and refold a road map at the same time.

Aeroma
(ayr oh' ma)

n. The odour emanating from an exercise room after an aerobics workout.

Aeropalmics
(ayr o palm' iks)

n. The study of wind resistance conducted by holding a cupped hand out the car window.

Age of Clausability
(ayj' uv klaw' za bil' ih tee)

n. The point at which we stop believing in Santa.

Aircapped
(ayr' capt)

v. To be temporarily crippled when the aeroplane passenger in front of you drives his seat back into your knees.

Airdirt
(ayr' dirt)

n. A hanging plant that's been ignored for three weeks or more.

Airpunt
(ayr' punt)

n. Any of a series of kicks that advances one's baggage towards the airport counter.

Alfred Hitchcooking

(al' fred hich' cooh king)

v. Continuously stabbing at a block of frozen vegetables to make them cook faster.

Ambiportalous
(am bih port' ahl us)

adj. Possessing the uncanny knack for approaching a set of double doors and *always* pushing the locked one.

Anafondics
(an a fon' diks)

n. Exercising to a workout album at 16 RPM.

Anananany
(an a na' na nee)

n. The inability to stop spelling the word 'banana' once you've started.

Anchority
(an chor' ih tee)

n. A group's final, hard-fought decision on what toppings to order on a pizza.

Anticiparcellate
(an ti si par' sel ate)

v. Waiting until the postman is several houses down the street before picking up the mail, so as not to appear too anxious.

Applaflammaphobia
(ap la flam uh fo' bee uh)

n. Fear that upon departing for holiday, you've left an appliance on that will burn the house to the ground.

Aquacoustics

(ak wa koo' stiks)

n. Sound waves in the bathroom that enable anyone to sing on key.

Aquadextrous

(ak wa deks' trus)

adj. Possessing the ability to turn the bath tap on and off with your toes.

Arachnidiot

(ar ak ni' di ot)

n. A person, who, having wandered into an 'invisible' spider web, begins gyrating and flailing about wildly.

Aspirbayerperpair-perfection

(as pur bayr' pur payr' pur fek' shun)

n. The ability to always extract *exactly* two headache tablets from the bottle.

Asterexasper

(as tuhr eggs as' pur)

n. An asterisk with no corresponding footnote.

Auldlanxiety

(old lang zi' et ee)

n. Experience of waking up on New Year's Day and wondering how much of a fool you made of yourself.

Awslice

(aww' slice)

n. The first slice of a wedding cake. The one which ruins the design and causes everyone to sigh.

azu ~

Azugos

(as' you goes)

n. Items to be carried upstairs by the next ascending person.

B

Backspubble

(bak' spuh bul)

n. Dishwater that disappears down one drain of a double sink and comes up the other.

Baldage

(bald' aj)

n. The accumulation of hair in the plug after showering.

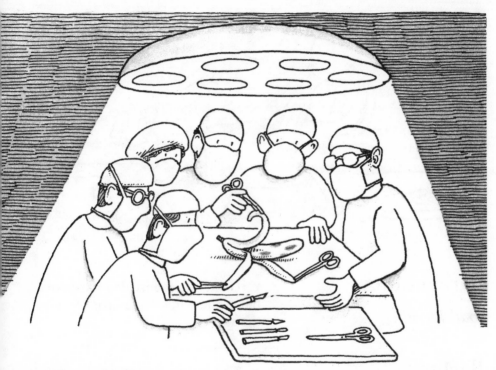

Banectomy

(bah nek' to mee)

n. The removal of bruises on a banana.

Barbalysis

(bar ba' lih sis)

n. Condition that arises from having to keep your head motionless while getting a haircut.

Barcuuming

(bar' ku ming)

v. Using the family dog to remove the crumbs that have dropped to the floor.

Barfium

(bar' fee um)

n. The horrible smelling cleanser they mop down school corridors with.

Bargus

(bar' jus)

n. The area on the windscreen that the wipers can't reach.

Bathquake

(bath' kwake)

n. The violent quake that rattles the entire house when the water tap is turned to a certain point.

Bazookacidal Tendencies

(bah zew' kuh sy dal ten' den seez)

n. The overwhelming desire of most individuals to reach out and pop the gigantic gum bubble billowing from someone's mouth.

Beavo
(bee' vo)

n. A pencil with teeth marks all over it.

Bimp
(bimp)

n. A blurry or 'double-edged' felt-tip marker.

Bixplex
(biks' pleks)

n. Psychological block in which a person cannot choose which colour of disposable lighter to purchase.

Bleemus
(blee' mus)

n. The disgusting film on the top of soups and cocoa that sit out for too long.

Blibula
(blih' byu luh)

n. The spot on a dog's stomach which, when rubbed, causes his leg to rotate wildly.

Blindelize
(blin' dul eyes)

v. To scratch an album beyond recognition trying to manoeuvre it over the record spindle.

Blisterpeg

(blys' tur peg)

n. The irritating part of a thong or flip flop that holds your foot on.

Blithwapping

(blith' wap ing)

v. Using anything BUT a hammer to hammer a nail into the wall, such as shoes, lamp base, doorstops, etc.

Blivett

(blih' vit)

v. To turn one's pillow over and over, looking for the cool spot.

Blog

(blog)

n. Overly generous deposits of fish food floating at the top of an aquarium.

Blotch

(blohch)

v. To slap the bottom of a ketchup bottle with increasing intensity, ultimately resulting in BLOTCHSLIDE.

Blurfle

(bler' ful)

v. To be caught talking at the top of one's voice when the music at the bar or disco suddenly stops.

bob ~

Bobblogesture

(boh blo jes' cher)

n. The classroom activity of not knowing an answer but raising one's hand anyway (after determining a sufficient number of other people have also raised their hands, thus reducing the likelihood of actually being called on).

Bomca

(bohm' ka)

n. A lubricant derived from the salivary gland used for turning book pages.

Bovilexia

(bo vil eks' e uh)

n. The uncontrollable urge to lean out the car window and yell 'Moo!!' every time you pass a cow.

Brattled

(brat' uld)

adj. The unsettling feeling, at a traffic light, that the busload of kids that just pulled up beside you is making fun of you.

Brazel

(brah' zul)

n. The scratch plate on a matchbook.

Brimplet

(brim' plit)

n. A frayed shoelace that must be moistened to pass through a shoe eyelet.

Broop

(broop)

n. The useless pocket on a pyjama top.

Bubblic

(buh' blik)

adj. Addicted to the systematic popping of the bubbles in packing material.

Bugpedal

(bug' ped uhl)

v. To accelerate or decelerate rapidly in an attempt to remove a clinging insect from a car's windscreen.

Burbulation

(ber byu lay' shun)

n. The obsessive act of opening and closing a refrigerator door in an attempt to catch it before the little automatic light comes on.

Burgacide

(burg' uh side)

n. When a hamburger can't take any more torture and hurls itself through the grill into the coals.

bur ~

Burgatory
(ber' ga tawr ee)

n. The place where unsold burgers go when the stand shuts down for the night.

Bursploot
(ber' sploot)

· To position one's thumb at the end of a garden hose to increase the water pressure.

Butthenge
(but' henj)

n. A pile of cigarette butts occupying a parking space.

Buttnick
(but' nik)

n. The crevice on an ashtray where the cigarette rests.

Buttras
(but' ruhs)

n. Those small buttons in a plastic bag that accompany finer clothing.

C

Cabnicreep

(kab' nih kreep)

n. The structural condition in which the closing of one kitchen cabinet causes another to open.

Caltitude

(kal' tih tood)

n. The height to which a cat's rear end can rise to meet the hand stroking it.

car ~

Carperimeter
(kar pur ihm' ih tur)

n. The zone between the wall and the end of the vacuum cleaner where dirt is 'safe'.

Carperpetuation
(kar' pur pet u a shun)

n. The act, when vacuuming, of running over a string or a piece of cotton at least a dozen times, reaching over and picking it up, examining it, then putting it back down to give the vacuum *one more chance*.

Carpillary Action
(kar' pih ler ee ak' shun)

n. Property that enables water to move up a windscreen when the vehicle is in motion.

Catlapse
(kat' laps)

n. The amount of time a cat sleeping on his owner's lap has to awake and prepare to hit the floor before the owner stands up.

Chalktrauma
(chawk' traw ma)

n. The body's reaction to someone running his fingernails down a blackboard.

Checkuary

(chek' yew air ee)

n. The thirteenth month of the year. Begins New Year's Day and ends when a person stops absentmindedly writing the old year on his cheques.

Choconiverous

(chok o niv' ur us)

adj. The tendency when eating a chocolate Easter bunny to bite off the head first.

cho ~

Choctasy
(chok' ta see)

n. The joy of discovering a second layer of chocolates underneath the first.

Chronesia
(kron ee' zyuh

n. The tendency not to know the time when asked, even though you've just looked at your watch.

Chubble
(chuh' bul)

n. The aerobic movement combining deep-knee bends and sideward hops used when trying to fit into tights.

Chwads
(chwadz)

n. The small, disgusting wads of chewed gum commonly found beneath table and counter tops.

Cigadent
(sig' a dent)

n. Any accident involving a cigarette: for instance when it sticks to your lips while your fingers slide off and get burned.

Cineplegic

(sih neh plee' jik)

n. A person whose foot has temporarily lost circulation from being wedged between theatre seats.

Circlocryogenic Theory

(sur klo kri o jen' ik the' uh ree)

n. Postulates that no matter which way you turn a glass of water, the ice cubes will move to the back. (Further research has established that one piece of ice will always stick to the bottom of an empty glass until tapped, at which point it will come forward and smack the drinker on the end of his nose.)

Circuloin Technique

(sur' kew loyn tek neek')

n. The popular approach to steak eating in which one eats around the edges first, then works his way toward the middle.

Circumvaculate

(sur kum vak' yew layt)

v. To remain stationary while vacuuming in a circle around oneself.

Clumfert

(klum' furt)

n. The invisible extra step at the top and bottom of a staircase. Usually materializes when one is carrying a large bag of groceries.

Coeggulant

(ko eg' yu lent)

n. The white things in a plate of scrambled eggs.

Coinophony

(koy' noh foh nee)

n. Annoying pocket concerts conducted by people who like to jingle keys and loose change, often accompanied by a rocking motion.

Combiloops

(kom' bih lewps)

n. The two or three unsuccessful passes before finally opening a combination locker.

Comeondowns

(kum on downz')

n. Depression resulting from knowing all the answers to a game show while confined in your living room.

The Cranial Stomp

(the kray' nee uhl stomp)

n. A somewhat primitive dance performed by youngsters trying to step on the heads of their shadows.

Crayollia

(kray oh' lee uh)

n. The area on the refrigerator where children's drawings are displayed.

Creedles

(kre' dulz)

n. The colony of microscopic indentations on a golf ball.

cri ~

Crinks

(krinks)

n. Crevices and junctions where car wax gets in but doesn't get out.

Crumbplumb

(krum' plum)

v. To attack a cereal box in an attempt to retrieve the prize.

Crummox

(krum' oks)

n. The cereal that gets caught between the inner lining and the side of the box. Also, the leftover amount at the bottom. (Not enough to eat, but too much to throw away.)

Crustadjuster

(krus' ta jus tur)

n. The 'light-dark' knob on a toaster that makes you think you're in control.

Cubelo

(kyew' beh lo)

n. The one cube left by the person too lazy to refill the ice tray.

Cubestacle

(kewb' stack ul)

n. A person who, no matter where he stands, gets in the way of someone playing pool.

cuf ~

Cufflatch
(kuf' lach)

v. To grasp the edge of one's sleeve to keep it from slithering up the arm while pulling on a sports jacket.

Curodds
(kur' ohds)

n. The adhesive plasters at the bottom of the box designed for extremely unusual injuries.

Cushup
(kush' up)

v. To sit down on a couch somehow causing the cushion next to you to rise.

D

Darf
(darf)

n. The least attractive side of a Christmas tree that ends up facing the wall.

Dasho
(da' show)

n. The area between a car's windscreen and dashboard, where coins, pencils, etc cannot be humanly retrieved.

Deterrency

(de ter' ren see)

n. The ruined currency found in trouser pockets after washing.

Detruncus

(de trunk' us)

n. The embarrassing phenomenon of losing one's bathing trunks while diving into a swimming pool.

Diagonerd

(dy ag' oh nurd)

n. Person who angles his car across two spaces to keep people from parking too close.

Digitritus

(dij ih tree' tus)

n. Deposits found between the links of a watchstrap.

Dillrelict

(dil rel' ikt)

n. The last pickle in the jar that avoids all attempts to be captured.

dim ~

Dimp
(dimp)

n. A person who insults you in a cheap department store by asking 'do you work here?'.

Dipwavers
(dip' way vurz)

n. People who raise their hands when riding on roller coasters.

Disconfect
(dis kon fekt')

v. To sterilize the sweet you dropped on the floor by blowing on it, somehow assuming this will 'remove' all the germs.

Doork
(dawrk)

n. A person who always pushes a door marked 'pull' or vice versa.

Door Slinky
(dor slin' kee)

n. The springy device attached to the back of a door that prevents the door from marring the wall.

Downpause
(down' pawz)

n. The split second of dry weather experienced when driving through an underpass during a storm.

Drylowgraphs

(dry' loh grafs)

n. Strange, unintelligible symbols that accompany the washing instructions on clothing labels.

dub ~

Dublectate

(duh blek' tayt)

v. To misplace one's glasses and eventually discover them on top of one's head.

E

Ectolacto

(ek toh lak' toh)

n. That curtain of milk that runs down the outside of the glass when you try to pour it into the cereal bowl.

Eggory

(eg' er ee)

n. The part of the fridge that holds the eggs.

Eiffelites

(eye' ful eyetz)

n. Gangly people sitting in front of you at the cinema who, no matter what direction you lean in, follow suit.

Elbonics
(el bon' iks)

n. The actions of two people manoeuvring for one armrest in a cinema.

Elecelleration
(el a cel er ay' shun)

n. The mistaken notion that the more you press a lift button the faster it will arrive.

Elemeno
(LMNO)

n. The centremost letter in the alphabet. The one that reduces it from twenty-six characters to twenty-three.

Elevertigo
(el uh vur' tig oh)

n. The sensation one experiences when a lift stops or takes off too suddenly.

Erdu
(uhr' dew)

n. The leftover accumulation of rubber particles after erasing a mistake on a test paper.

Escalasticize

(esk a last' i size)

v. To lean against the rail of a moving escalator and have the sensation of being pulled in opposite directions.

Essoasso

(es oh as' oh)

n. A person who cuts through a petrol station to avoid a red light.

Exaspirin

(eks as' prin)

n. Any bottle of pain reliever with an impossible-to-remove cotton wad at the top.

Execuglide

(eks ek' yew glyd)

v. To propel oneself about an office without getting up from the chair. Best results achieved when using a typist's chair.

exp ~

Expressholes
(eks pres' holz)

n. People who try to sneak more than the 'eight items or less' into the express checkout line.

Eufirstics
(yew fur' stiks)

n. Two people waiting on the phone for the other to hang up first.

F

Falooter
(fa lew' tur)

n. The rope running through a menu that lets you know you're at a fancy restaurant.

Famamage
(fa mam' aj)

v. To eliminate any annoying engine noise by simply turning up the volume of the radio.

Farrelphobia
(fayr el foh' bee yuh)

n. Fear of being approached by several dozen waiters singing 'Happy Birthday'.

Feasers

(fee' zurz)

n. The racing stripes on tennis shoes that fool kids into thinking they can run faster.

Ferroles

(fer' olz)

n. The holes in the bottom of a steam iron.

Fetchplex

(fech' pleks)

n. State of momentary confusion in a dog whose owner has faked throwing the ball and palmed it behind his back.

fic ~

Fictate
(fik' tayt)

v. To inform a television or screen character of impending danger under the assumption they can hear you.

Firssue
(fur' shew)

n. The lead tissue. The one that gets all the others going.

Flarpswitch
(flarp' swich)

n. The one light switch in every house with no function whatsoever.

Fleabage
(flee' baj)

n. Excess of flea collar that has to be cut off.

Flen
(flen)

n. (Chemical symbol: Fl) The black crusty residue that accumulates on the necks of old ketchup bottles.

Fleptic
(flep' tik)

adj. The tendency of soup and dog food lids to slip into the can upon opening.

Flirr
(flur)

n. A photograph that features the camera operator's finger in the corner.

Flotion
(flo' shun)

n. The tendency when sharing a waterbed to undulate for five minutes every time the other person moves.

Flurrant
(fluhr' uhnt)

n. The one leaf that always clings to the end of the rake.

Fods
(fohdz)

n. Couples at amusement parks who wear identical T-shirts, presumably to keep from getting lost.

Foomlet
(foom' lit)

n. The bathroom towel you're not allowed to use because it's marked 'guest', and guests don't use because who wants to be the first person to mess it up?

Foopers

(foo' perz)

n. Passers-by at restaurant windows who stop to watch you eat.

Foys

(foyz)

n. Missing pieces of a jigsaw puzzle that you later find stuck to the underside of your arm.

Fraznit

(frahs' nit)

n. Any string hanging from an article of clothing, which when pulled causes the article to unravel completely.

Frust

(frust)

n. The small line of debris that refuses to be swept onto the dust pan and keeps backing a person across the room until he finally decides to give up and sweep it under the rug.

Fuffle

(fuh' ful)

v. To assume, when dining out, that you are making things easier on the waitress by using the phrase 'when you get a chance ...'.

Furnidents

(fer' nih dents)

n. The indentations that appear in carpets after a piece of furniture has been removed.

G

Gangloot

(gan' glewt)

n. Person who leaves all his ski passes on his jacket just to impress people.

Garbpaction
(garb pak' shun)

n. The act of cramming just one more item into a rubbish bin to avoid emptying it.

Garmites
(gar' mitz)

n. Those items of clothing that fit perfectly in the store, but somehow shrink on the way home.

Gazinta (÷)
(gah zin' tuh)

n. Mathematical symbol for division; also the sound uttered when dividing out loud. (Example ('Four *gazinta* eight twice.')

Geouch
(jee' owch)

n. The sharp rock one always finds directly beneath his sleeping bag.

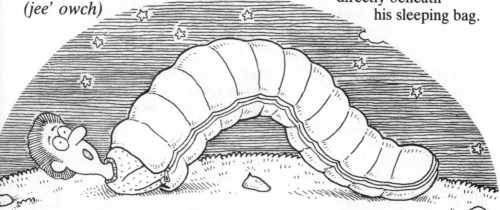

Gertatious

(gur tay' shus)

adj. Having the adolescent fear that hanging one's arm over the bed at night will mean being dragged under.

Gibble

(jib' buhl)

n. The sliding keyhole cover on a car boot.

Glamp
(glamp)

n. The telescopic device used to retrieve golf balls from ponds.

Glantics
(glan' tiks)

n. Two people who, while kissing, open their eyes at the same time to see if the other is looking.

Gleemule
(glee' mule)

n. (a unit of measure) One unit of toothpaste, measured from bristle to bristle. (Not to be confused with GLEEMITES, which are petrified deposits of toothpaste found in sinks.)

Grackles
(grak' elz)

n. The wrinkles that appear on the body after staying in water too long.

Grantnap
(grant' nap)

n. The extra five minutes of sleep you allow yourself that somehow makes all the difference in the world.

gre ~

Greedling
(gree' dling)

v. Pretending to read the inscription on the birthday card when you really just want to know how much it costs.

Greepers
(greep' ers)

n. People who walk up the down escalator in an attempt to appear motionless.

Grinion
(grin' yun)

n. The unsightly indentation in the middle of a belt when it has been worn too long.

Grintiger
(grin' tuh jer)

n. The numbered code on the back of a greeting card that, when deciphered, reveals the price.

Gunkoleum
(gun koh' lee yum)

n. The horrible black paste that car manufacturers smear under car seats.

Gymbols
(jim' bolz)

n. Those lines and markings on a gym floor that have no purpose whatsoever.

H

Hacula

(hak' yew luh)

n. The last few inches of tape measure or lawn mower cord that refuse to rewind automatically.

Halvent

(hav' ent)

n. A style of car window, found in later models, that only rolls down halfway.

Hangle

(han' gul)

n. A cluster of coat hangers.

Hemoplugs

(hee' moh plugz)

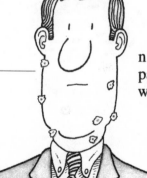

n. Small pieces of toilet paper applied to shaving wounds.

Houndwounding

(hownd' wown ding)

n. Canine act of circling a spot three or four times before settling on it.

Hozone
(ho' zohn)

n. The place where one sock in every laundry load disappears to.

Hudnut
(hud' nut)

n. The bolt left over when one has finished reassembling a bicycle or car engine.

Hydralation

(hi dra lay' shun)

n. Acclimatizing oneself to a cold swimming pool by bodily regions: toe-to-knee, knee-to-waist, waist-to-elbow, elbow-to-neck.

Hystioblogination

(his' te o blog in ay' shun)

n. The act of trying to identify a gift by holding it to your ear and shaking the parcel.

I

Icision

(ih sih' zhun)

n. Delicate operation performed on Neapolitan-flavoured ice cream in which one entire flavour is precisely and systematically removed.

Idiot Box

(id' e ot bohks)

n. The part of the envelope that tells a person *where* to place the stamp when they can't quite figure it out for themselves.

Ignisecond

(ig' ni sek und)

n. The overlapping moment of time when the hand is locking the car door even as the brain is saying 'my keys are in there!'.

Illuminot

(il ew' mih noht)

n. Device in aeroplane bathrooms that won't let the light come on until you lock the door.

Impassengers

(im pas' enj urz)

n. Two people, one inside the car, one outside, negating each other's actions while trying to unlock the door.

Inelvitable

(in el' vih tuh bul)

adj. The uncanny ability of a band in old Elvis Presley movies to materialize from nowhere whenever Elvis begins to sing.

Inknition

(ink nih' shun)

n. The metal clicker at the top of a cheap ball point pen that: a) puts it into operation and b) is also perfect for driving substitute teachers crazy.

Inkslick

(ink' slik)

n. A greasy spot on a piece of stationery or test paper.

Irant

(eye' rant)

n. A seamless pistachio nut; a pistachio nut afraid to come out in public.

J

Javajetsam
(ja va jet' sum)

n. Washed ashore coffee grounds on the rim of the cup.

Jukejitters
(jook' jit erz)

n. Fear that everyone thinks you picked the awful tune emanating from the jukebox when it was actually the person before you.

K

Kawashock
(kah wah shohk')

n. Pulling into the last remaining parking spot only to discover a motorcycle there.

Keyfruit

(kee' froot)

n. The one apple, pear, or tomato in the stand that, when removed, causes all the others to tumble forward.

key ~

Keylonius
(key loan' ee us)

adj. The slight trace of criminality one feels when having one's keys duplicated.

Knimpel
(nim' pul)

n. The missing last piece of a jigsaw puzzle.

Krogling
(kroh' gling)

n. The nibbling of small items of fruit and produce at the supermarket, which the customer considers 'free sampling' and the owner considers 'shoplifting'.

L

Lactomangulation
(lak' to man gyu lay' shun)

n. Manhandling the 'open here' spout on a milk carton so badly that one has to resort to using the 'illegal side'.

Lexicaves
(leks' ih kayuz)

n. Indentations on the side of a dictionary.

Lexplexed
(leks' plekst)

adj. Unable to find the correct spelling for a word in the dictionary because you don't know how to spell it.

Linenarctica
(lin en ark' tik uh)

n. The corner of the bed that is impossible to reach when putting on new sheets.

Lintulyptus
(lin tu lip' tus)

n. Any cough sweet found in one's pocket after a long period of time.

Litmusload
(lit' mus lode)

n. Any washload that comes out the colour of the one item that faded.

Loggium
(log' yum)

n. Water that drips from one's nose hours after swimming.

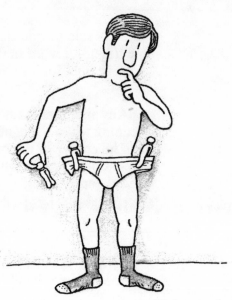

Loomlies

(lewm' leez)

n. Y-fronts that have lost their elasticity.

Lorp

(lawrp)

n. The part of the shoe that collapses when you try to pull it on without a shoehorn.

Lub

(lub)

n. The small deposit of spinach that lodges itself between one's teeth.

M

Magnagram

(mag' nuh gram)

n. Any sign that takes on a new meaning when a magnetic letter falls off.

Maltian

(mal' shun)

n. The alien beside you with concave cheeks, bulging forehead veins, and clearly outlined skull who is sucking on a too thick milk shake.

Manglazette

(mang la zet')

n. The newspaper at the top of the stack that everyone passes over, believing the ones beneath it have better or fresher news.

Manumulching

(man' yew mul ching)

v. Transporting leaves by sandwiching them between one hand and the rake.

Marp

(marp)

n. The impossible-to-find beginning of a roll of sticky tape.

Mattrescotting

(mat' res kot ing)

n. The pattern of grey and white lines on an institutional mattress.

Maytag Massage

(may' tag muh sahj')

n. The momentary thrill experienced while sitting on a washing machine as it launches into the spin cycle.

med ~

Medipeep

(meh' dee peep)

n. Uncontrollable urge to look inside a host's bathroom cabinet to see what kind of afflictions he suffers from.

Meganegabar

(meg uh neg' uh bar)

n. The line you draw across the 'amount' section of a cheque to prevent people from adding, 'and a million pounds'.

Memomimicry

(mem oh mim' ih kree)

n. The brief lapse in a phone conversation where you pretend to be getting a pencil to write down an important message.

Memosphere
(meh' moh sfeer)

n. The part of the sky one searches when trying to recall something in the past.

Merferator
(mur' fur ay ter)

n. The cardboard core in a toilet roll.

Methylphobia
(meth il fo' be uh)

n. The fear that you are going to have to pay for the one penny you over-pumped at the self-service petrol station.

Microtrek
(my' kro trek)

n. Any nervous trip to the microwave oven to make sure the food hasn't incinerated.

Microts
(my' krotz)

n. The two thumbnail-sized pieces you end up with when trying to remove a paper towel in a public washroom.

Miniblurb
(mih' nee blerb)

n. That useless piece of information about the author found on the back of a book.

Miscordance

(mis kawr' dans)

n. The principle that states: when reaching for curtain cords, you will always tug on the wrong one first, practically tearing down the whole contraption.

Mommenoia

(mom muh noy' ah)

n. Fear that the dentist or doctor will barge in and catch you playing with his equipment.

Motmeshs

(moht' mesh ez)

n. A pair of inseparable shopping trolleys.

Motodrift

(moh' toh drift)

n. The mistaken belief at a traffic light that your car is moving backward when, actually, the car beside you is moving forward.

Motspur

(mot' sper)

n. The pesky fourth wheel on a shopping trolley that refuses to cooperate with the other three.

Mowmuffins

(mo' muh finz)

n. The dried accumulation of grass on the underside of lawnmowers.

Mozzalastics

(moht suh las' tiks)

n. Large deposits of cheese that stick to the top of the pizza box.

Mugpuddles

(mug' pud ulz)

n. Small bodies of water that collect on upturned mugs in the dishwasher.

Multipochoholes

(mul ti po' cho holz)

n. Wounds left in test papers from overerasing.

Mummabolic Chorus

(mum uh boh' lik ko' rus)

n. When three or more people are singing along to a tune and suddenly discover they are all faking their way through the unintelligible lyrics.

Mumphreys

(mum' freez)

n. (a useless sniglet) Those strange extra digits you find on push-button phones.

Mustgo

(must' go)

n. Any item of food that has been sitting in the refrigerator so long it has become a science project.

N

Napjerk

(nap' jurk)

n. The sudden convulsion of the body just as one is about to doze off.

Narcolepulacy

(nar ko lep' ul ah see)

n. The contagious action of yawning, causing everyone else in sight also to yawn.

Negatile

(neh' guh tyl)

n. An area of the bathroom floor where, somehow, the scales register you five pounds lighter.

Neonphancy

(ne on' fan see)

n. A fluorescent light bulb struggling to come to life.

Nerkle

(nur' kel)

n. A person who leaves his Christmas lights up all year.

Nevitts

(nev' itz)

n. The sandpaper-like deposits on a cat's tongue.

Nicometeor

(nik oh mee' tee awr)

n. A cigarette that exits through a car's front window and re-enters through the back.

Nifleck

(nih' flek)

n. The unmarked domino in the set.

nin ~

Ninker
(nin' ker)

n. Any utensil that positions itself inside a drawer to prevent the drawer from opening.

Nistols
(niz' tolz)

n. The small rubbery pads on the bottom of a dog's paw.

Nitvwit
(nit' vwit)

n. Any person who can't find reverse gear in a Volkswagen.

Niz
(niz)

n. An annoying hair at the top of a cinema screen.

Nocturnuggets
(nok' ter nuh gitz)

n. Deposits found in one's eye upon awakening in the morning, also called: GOZZAGAREENA, OPTIGOOK, EYEHOCKEY, etc.

Noflet

(nahf' lit)

n. The upward swirl of hair found on certain individuals such as Ronald Reagan.

Nozzlop

(noz' zlop)

n. To look into a garden hose to see if the water is coming.

Nurge

(nerj)

v. To inch closer to a traffic light thinking that will cause it to change quicker.

O

Oatgap

(oht' gap)

n. The empty space in a cereal box created by 'settling during shipment'.

110 at the Equator

(won' ten at the ek way' tawr)

n. Any burning sensation experienced directly below the navel when putting on a pair of jeans straight from the dryer.

Oopzama

(ewp' za muh)

n. Sudden scratching of scalp or face upon realization that the person you were waving at isn't who you thought it was.

Opling

(oh' pling)

n. The act, when feeding a baby, of opening and closing one's mouth, smacking one's lips and making 'yummy' noises, in the hope that baby will do the same.

Optortionist

(op tor' shun ist)

n. The kid in school who can turn his eyelids inside out.

Opup
(op' uhp)

v. To push one's glasses back on the nose.

Orogami
(or oh ga' mee)

n. The miraculous folding process that allows Kleenexes to emerge methodically from the box one at a time.

Orqo
(oar' ko)

n. The small bar that turns an 'O' into a 'Q.'

Otisosis
(oh tis oh' sis)

n. The inability to meet anyone else's eyes in a lift.

P

Parsleyvania
(par slee vay' nyuh)

n. The place where all the fancy restaurant garnish that is never eaten comes from.

pas ~

Pastaplegic
(pas tuh plee' jik)

n. Person who's eaten so much spaghetti he can't move.

Payfall
(pay' fal)

n. The phone booth sound that tricks you into thinking your coin has accidentally returned.

Pedaeration
(ped air ay' shun)

n. Perfect body heat achieved by having one leg under the sheet and one hanging off the edge of the bed.

Pediddel
(pe did' ul)

n. A car with only one working headlight. (*Related to* LEDDIDEP: a car with only one working taillight.)

Pedlock
(ped' lohk)

n. The condition of a bicycle pedal wedging itself against the kickstand.

Peepola
(pee poe' luh)

n. The gap in the dressing room curtain that can never be completely closed.

Pelp
(pelp)

n. The crumbs and food particles that accumulate in the cracks of dining tables.

Pencicopter
(pen' sih kop tur)

n. Classroom invention fashioned from a pencil and a ruler during periods of extreme boredom.

Penciventilation
(pen si ven ti lay' shun)

n. The act of blowing on the tip of a pencil after sharpening it.

Peppiér
(pehp ee ay')

n. The waiter at a fancy restaurant whose sole purpose seems to be walking around asking diners if they want ground pepper.

Pepsilluvium
(pep sil lew' vee yum)

n. The tiny amount of cola that escapes when you push a straw through the lid of a soft drink.

Percambulate
(pur kam' byew layt)

v. Tendancy of fitted sheets to lose their grip and roll up the mattress.

Percuburp

(per' kyu berp)

n. The final gasp a coffee percolator makes to alert you it is ready.

Permapression

(pur' muh preh shun)

n. The discovery that there is no real difference in the various cycles of your washing machine.

Petonic

(peh ton' ik)

adj. One who is embarrassed to undress in front of a household pet.

Phistel

(fis' tul)

n. The brake pedal on the passenger side of the car that you wish existed when you're riding with a lunatic.

Phonesia

(fo nee' zhuh)

n. The affliction of dialing a phone number and forgetting whom you were calling just as they answer.

Photoyokel

(fo to yo' kul)

n. A person who presses the wrong button on a film camera causing it to dismantle.

Phosflink

(fos' flink)

v. To flick a bulb on and off when it burns out (as if, somehow, that will bring it back to life).

Phozzle

(fo' zul)

n. The build-up of dust on a record needle.

Pielibrium

(py lih' bree uhm)

n. The point at which the crust on a wedge of pie outweighs the filling and tips it over.

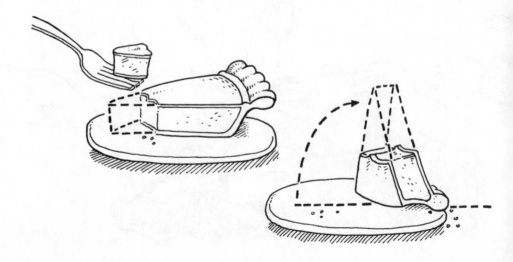

Piewagon

(py' wa gun)

n. The small vehicle that carries game pieces around a Trivial Pursuit board.

Pifflesquit

(pif' ul skwit)

n. The wire net surrounding the cork of a champagne bottle.

Pigslice

(pig' slys)

n. The last unclaimed piece of pizza that everyone is secretly dying for.

pil ~

Pillsburglar

(pilz' berg ler)

n. Person able to sample the icing on a new cake without leaving a fingerprint.

Pockalanche

(pok' uh lansh)

n. Perpetual action of reaching down to pick up an item fallen from a shirt pocket, only to have another item fall out.

Polarind

(poh' luh rynd)

n. The peeling on a Polaroid snapshot.

Porcelator

(pawr' suh lay tawr)

n. The hole near the rim of a bathroom sink.

Postalports

(poh' stuhl pawrtz)

n. The annoying windows in envelopes that never line up with the address.

Premaderci

(pree muh dayr' chi)

n. The act of saying goodbye to someone, then running into him again moments later (usually accompanied by a lame quip such as 'you following me?').

Premail

(pree' mayl)

n. Mail that is placed behind the visor in the car and left for several months before it is finally sent.

pri ~

Primpo
(prim' po)

n. A person who passes a mirror then has to step back, presumably to reassure himself he still exists.

Profanitype
(pro fan' i tipe)

n. The special symbols used by cartoonists to replace swear words (points, asterisks, stars, and so on). It is yet to be determined which specific character represents which specific expletive.

P-spot
(pee' spoht)

n. The area directly above the urinal in public washrooms that men stare at, knowing a glance in any other direction would arouse suspicion.

Psychophobia
(sy ko fo' be uh)

n. The compulsion, when using a host's bathroom, to peer behind the shower curtain and make sure no one is waiting for you.

Pulpsqulpgulp
(pulp' skulp gulp)

v. To slurp the grapefruit juice straight from the bowl it's served in and abandon all civility.

Pupkus

(pup' kus)

n. The moist residue left on a window after a dog presses its nose to it.

Pupsqueak

(puhp' skweek)

n. The sound a yawning dog emits when it opens its mouth too wide.

Purcilious

(per sil' ee us)

adj. The manner in which a man holds his wife's handbag in public, as if it contained some odious matter.

Purpitation

(per pi tay' shun)

v. To take something off the grocery shelf, decide you don't want it, and then put it in another section.

pyj ~

Pyjangle

(pye jan' gul)

n. Condition of waking up with your pyjamas turned 180 degrees.

R

Rampriot

(ramp' ry uht)

n. Free-for-all that erupts as soon as the stewardess utters the phrase 'please remain in your seats until the plane has come to a complete stop'.

Reled

(ree led')

v. To reset all the digital clocks in the household following a power failure.

Reyulerate

(re yew' lur ayt)

v. To reposition Christmas tree lights so no two of the same colours are beside each other.

Riceroach

(rys' rohch)

n. The burnt krispie in every bowl of Rice Krispies.

Rignition
(rig ni' shun)

n. The embarrassing action of trying to start one's car with the engine already running.

Rocktose
(rok' tohs)

n. The hard lumps that block the pouring spouts of sugar dispensers.

Roebinks
(roh' binks)

n. Those mysterious chimes you always hear in department stores.

Rohrshirt
(roar' shurt)

n. A shirt with an ink stain on the pocket.

Rovalert
(ro' val urt)

n. The system whereby one dog can quickly establish an entire neighbourhood network of barking.

Rubbage
(ruh' bij)

n. Large pieces of lorry tyre found on the side of the road.

Rubuncles
(ru' bunk ulz)

n. The bumps on an uncooked chicken.

Rumphump
(rump' hump)

n. The seat on the school bus directly over the rear wheel.

S

Sark
(sark)

n. The marks left on one's ankle after wearing socks all day.

Scadink
(ska' dink)

n. The annoying build-up of ink on the end of a ball-point pen.

Schlattwhapper
(shlat' wap ur)

n. The window blind that allows itself to be pulled down, hesitates for a second, then snaps up in your face.

Schnuffel

(shnuf' ul)

n. A dog's practice of continuously nuzzling your crotch in mixed company.

Schwiggle

(shwi' gul)

n. The amusing rotation of one's bottom while sharpening a pencil.

Scotchrotor

(skoch' roh tur)

n. The wheel left behind when all the sticky tape is used up.

Scribblics

(skrih' bliks)

n. Warm-up exercises designed to get the ink in a pen flowing.

Scribline
(skrib' line)

n. The blank area on the back of credit cards where one's signature goes.

Second Oilpinion [to get a]
(seh' cund oyl pin' yun)

v. Checking a dipstick, wiping it off, then *rechecking* because you never 'trust' it the first time.

Servelence
(surv' lents)

n. The sudden lull in conversation that occurs at a table of diners when the food is served.

Shirtlop
(shurt' lohp)

n. The condition of a shirt that has been improperly buttoned.

Shocklet
(shohk' lit)

n. The seldom-used third hole on an electrical socket.

Showershroud

(show' ur shrowd)

n. Those hotel shower curtains that inexplicably wrap themselves around you while you shower.

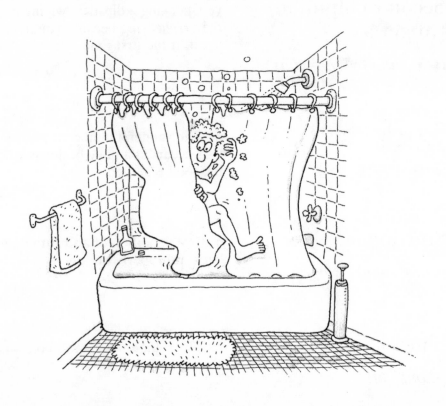

Shuggleftulation

(shug lef tuyl ay' shun)

n. The actions of two people approaching, trying to get around each other, and muttering 'thanks for the dance'.

Sirlines

(sir' lines)

n. The lines on a grilled steak.

Sizzlage

(siz' lidge)

n. The amount of skin one is willing to sacrifice while testing an iron to make sure it won't burn one's shirt.

Skivlines

(skiv' lynz)

n. The red or blue lines around boxer shorts that make them resemble fine china.

Slackjam

(slak' jam)

n. The condition of being trapped in one's own trousers while trying to pull them on without first removing shoes.

Sloopage

(slu' paj)

n. The tendency of hot dogs, hamburgers, and sandwich contents to slip from between their covers.

Sloovers

(sloo' vurz)

n. Remnants of soap too small to use, but too big to throw away.

Slopweaver

(slohp' wee vuhr)

n. Someone who has mastered the art of repositioning the food on his plate to give the appearance of having consumed a good portion of it.

Slottery and Vendication

(slot' er ee and ven' di kay shun)

n. A public misdemeanour in which a person gambles on a slot machine, loses, and tries to exact revenge by kicking it.

Sloverture

(slow' vur chur)

n. The distorted music which begins every educational film.

Slurch

(slerch)

n. The combination 'ouch' and slurping noise one makes when eyeing someone else's bad sunburn.

Slurm

(slerm)

n. The slime that accumulates on the underside of a bar of soap when it sits in the dish too long.

Smugsticker

(smug' stik kur)

n. The price tag that normally intelligent people leave on their new car window for months.

Snabble

(sna' bul)

v. To attempt to use a sniglet while playing Scrabble.

Snargle

(snar' gul)

v. To lessen the visual impact of a horror movie by filtering it through one's fingers.

Snorfing

(snorf' ing)

n. The little game waitresses love to play of waiting until your mouth is full before sneaking up and asking, 'Is everything okay?'.

Snuggage

(snuh' gaj)

n. The act of retying both shoelaces when only one needed it.

Somnambapologist

(som nam ba pol' uh jist)

n. Person too polite to admit he was sleeping even when awakened at three in the morning.

Spagellum

(spa gel' um)

n. The loose strand on each forkful of spaghetti that beats one about the chin and whiskers.

Spirobits

(spy' ro bits)

n. The frayed bits of left-behind paper in a spiral notebook.

Spirtle

(spur' tul)

n. The fine stream from a grapefruit that always lands right in your eye.

Spood

(spewd)

n. Flat wooden 'spoon' that accompanies ice cream cups.

Spork
(spork)

n. The combination spoon/fork you find in fast food restaurants.

Sprout Lines
(sprowt lynz)

n. Visible lines at the bottom of trouser legs where the hems have been let down.

Spudrubble
(spud' ruhb uhl)

n. Unclaimed french fries at the bottom of a fast food bag.

Spumpspeed
(spump' speed)

n. The velocity achieved between speed bumps before having to slow down again.

Squanderprint
(skwan' duhr print)

n. Directions that try to make you use up a product faster than you normally would. (Eg: Apply shampoo. Lather. Rinse. Repeat.)

Squatflection
(skwat' flek shun)

n. The distorted reflection in a car window that makes you resemble a midget wrestler.

Squatic Diversion

(skwa' tik dy vur' zhun)

n. Any pretended activity that commands a dog owner's attention while the dog relieves itself on a neighbour's lawn.

Squigger

(skwig' uhr)

n. A tomato that explodes upon contact with a fork.

Squinchooing

(skwin chew' ing)

v. Staring up at the sun to expedite a sneeze.

Stoptional

(stop' shun ul)

n. Any stop sign in the middle of nowhere that no one pays attention to.

Stroodle

(stru' dul)

n. The annoying strand of cheese stretching from a slice of hot pizza to one's mouth.

str ~

Strumble

(strum' bul)

n. That invisible object you always pretend made you trip, when it was actually your own stupid clumsiness.

Subatomic Toasticles

(sub ah tom' ik toh' stik uhlz)

n. Tiny fragments of toast left behind in the butter.

Subnougate

(sub new' get)

v. To eat the bottom layer in a box of chocolates and carefully replace the top level, hoping no one will notice.

Sudsorian Calendar

(sudz oar' ee an ka' len dur)

n. Calendar used on soap operas which allows one day's events to be stretched over a three-week period.

Suzmosis

(suz moh' sis)

n. Mysterious disappearance of dishwater even when the sink is plugged airtight.

Swurlee

(swer' lee)

n. A playground swing wrapped impossibly out of reach.

T

Table Snorkeling

(tay' bul snawrk' ling)

n. Frantic gesticulations when one bites into hot food and has to take in air to cool it off.

Tatercrater

(tay' tur kray' tur)

n. Hole dug in mashed potatoes to keep the gravy in.

tel ~

Telecrastination

(tel e kras tin ay' shun)

n. The act of always letting the phone ring at least twice before you pick it up, even when you're only six inches away.

Televelocity

(teh leh veh la' sih tee)

n. The speed at which one tries to reach the phone before the answering machine comes on.

Teloustic

(tel oo' stik)

adj. The tendency for people to shout into the phone when calling long distance.

Testlice
(test' lys)

n. Those tiny bugs that invade your hair when you're taking an exam.

Thermalophobia
(thur muh lo fo' be uh)

n. The fear when showering that someone will sneak in, flush the toilet, and scald you to death.

Thrickle
(thri' kel)

n. The itch in the back of the throat which can't be scratched without making disgusting farmyard-type noises.

Thrub
(thrub)

n. The small web of skin between the thumb and index finger that makes us 0.0005% amphibian.

Tile Comet

(tyl kom' it)

n. Any streamer of toilet paper attached to your heel as you emerge from a public washroom.

Toastate

(tohs' tayt)

v. To impatiently pop toast up and down in the toaster, thus increasing the likelihood of burning it.

Toastiphobia

(toh stih foh' bee yuh)

n. Fear of putting a fork in the toaster even when it is unplugged because, somehow, the toaster 'remembers'.

Todlitter

(tod' lit ur)

n. Food debris under a high chair following an attempted feeding.

Toolcentric

(tewl sen' trik)

adj. Describes any tool that, when dropped, rolls to the exact centre of the car's underside.

tru ~

Trufitti
(truh fee' tee)

n. Washing instructions found on the backs of dirty trucks.

Tubloids
(tuhb' loydz)

n. Any periodical reserved for bathroom readings.

Tubswizzle
(tub' swih zuhl)

v. To slide oneself back and forth in the bath in order to mix the too hot water with the cooler water.

Tupperwarp

(tuh' pur warp)

n. Condition of Tupperware left in the microwave too long.

Twinch

(twinch)

n. The movement a dog makes with its head when it hears a high-pitched noise.

U

Uclipse
(yew' klips)

n. The dangerous arc into another lane made by drivers just before executing a turn.

Ufluation
(yu flu ay' shun)

n. The peculiar habit, when searching for a snack, of constantly returning to the refrigerator in the hope that something new will have materialized.

Uhflaw
(yu' flaw)

n. The one television tuned to a different channel in the bank of televisions at the electrical shop.

Ultimato
(ul tih may' toe)

n. The choise of eating your vegetables or going to bed without supper.

Umbrace
(uhm' brays)

n. The small strap that holds an umbrella in place.

Umbroglio
(um brol' yoh)

n. Any conflict with an umbrella on a windy day.

Unfare

(un fayr')

n. The money you owe the taxi driver before you've even moved a foot.

Unipea

(yew' ni pee)

n. A peanut with only one compartment.

Upuls

(yu' puls)

n. The blank pages at the beginning and end of books, presumably placed there so you can rewrite the ending.

Urmommerize

(yer mom' mer eyes)

v. To attempt to decipher *exactly* what an upset coach is mouthing on T.V.

V

Vacation Elbow

(vay kay' shun el' bo)

n. A condition that suddenly develops in a father's arm during a holiday trip that allows him to reach out and slap you from incredible distances.

Vegeludes

(vej' eh loodz)

n. Individual peas or kernels of corn that you end up chasing all over the plate.

W

Waftic

(wahf' tik)

adj. Describes any person in whose direction campfire or barbeque smoke always blows.

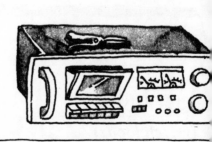

Warbloid

(war' bloyd)

n. The tiny device in cassette players that chews up tapes and spits them out in a mangled mess.

Wavoids

(way' voydz)

n. People who bob up and down in the ocean in time with the large waves in a vain attempt to stay dry above the waist.

Werdle

(wurd' uhl)

v. To lean over the edge of a train or tube platform in search of the oncoming vehicle. WERDLEMASS (n.)—an entire group of people leaning over a train or tube platform.

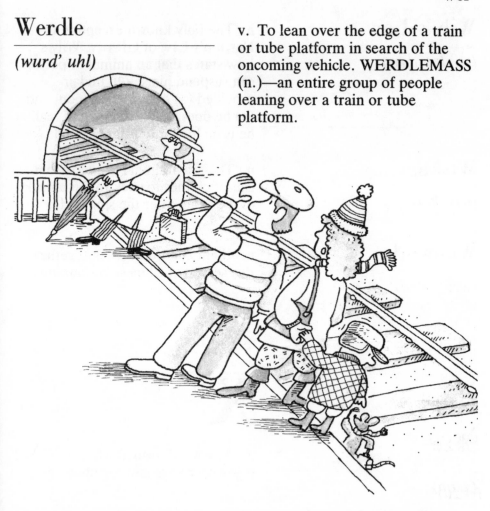

wil ~

Wily's Law

(wi' leez law)

n. The only known exception to Newton's Law of Gravity, Wily's Law states that an animal or person can suspend himself in midair provided (a) he is in a cartoon, and (b) he doesn't look down and realize he is no longer on solid ground.

Wiskage

(wis' kaj)

n. The gravitational property that causes clothes to stick to the outside of the drum after the spin cycle.

Woowad

(wew' wad)

n. Giant clumps of stuck-together rice served at Chinese restaurants.

X

Xleop Skzu

(xeop skzu)

n. Any word formed when typewriter keys jam together.

Xeroxpox
(zee' roks poks)

n. Skin disease of copier paper, characterized by the appearance of large black powdery blotches.

Xiidigitation
(ksi dij i tay' shun)

n. The practice of trying to determine the year a film was made by deciphering the roman numerals at the end of the credits.

Y

Yaffling
(yah' fling)

v. Speaking loudly to foreigners as if, somehow, this makes you easier to understand.

Yardribbons
(yard rib' onz)

n. The unmowed patches of grass discovered after one has put away the mower.

Yearagostats
(yeer' uh goh stats)

n. The part of a forecast that tells you what the weather was like a year ago so you'll feel even more miserable.

yin ~

Yinkel

(yin' kul)

n. A person who combs his hair over his bald spot, hoping no one will notice.

Yorange

(yawr' anj)

n. Those digusting white threads that hang from an orange after it has been peeled.

Yotate

(yoh' tayt)

n. To allow a yo-yo to unwind itself.

Z

Zebbits

(zeb' itz)

n. Those bizarre fireplace tools whose function no one seems able to explain.

Zimeter

(zi' me tur)

n. (a unit of measure) The last four or five inches of tape measure that never rewind automatically.

Zipcuffed
(zip' cuft)

v. To be trapped in one's trousers by a faulty zip.

Zippijig
(zih' pih jig)

n. The dance one performs whenever a rubber band is pointed at them.

Zizzebots
(zi' ze botz)

n. The marks on the bridge of one's nose visible when glasses are removed.

Zyxnoid
(ziks' noyd)

n. Any word that a crossword puzzler makes up to complete the last blank, accompanied by the rationalization that there probably is an ancient god named Ubbbu, or German river named Wfor, and besides, who's going to check?

Appendix A
Anatomical Sniglets

Chingrip *(chin' grip)*
n. Area where chin meets neck. Used for holding pillow when slipping on pillowcase.

Gimplexus *(gim plek' sis)*
n. Rear area of thighs, which must be peeled from car seat on hot summer days.

Glarpo *(glar' po)*
n. The juncture of the ear and skull where pencils are stored.

Gnarmblum *(narm' blum)*
n. The dry wrinkly area at the end of the elbow.

Gromaxes *(grom' ack sis)*
n. Inside area of knees used to grip steering wheel when holding a road map.

Nugloo *(nug' lew)*
n. Single continuous eyebrow that covers entire forehead.

Scrabitch *(skrab' ich)*
n. Impossible-to-reach area in middle of back which can never be scratched.

Sniffleridge *(snif' ul rij)*
n. Trough leading from the nose to upper lip.

Swazna *(swaz' nuh)*
n. The thin, digusting membrane that connects the bottom of the tongue to the top of the jaw, presumably to hold it in place.

Yink *(yinc)*
n. One strand of hair that covers bald spot.

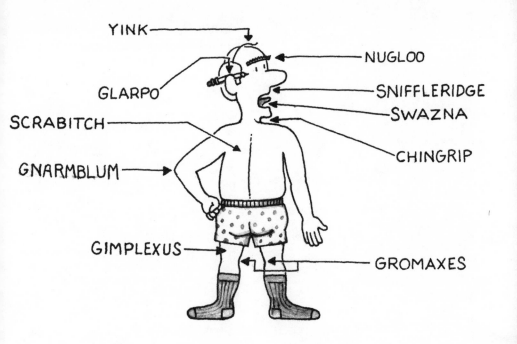